P&P

PRESS LTD

DEDICATION

In Memory

To Ron Coleman Snr

RIP

Ron Coleman & Mike Smith

February 2007

Foreword
Professor Marius Romme, Sandra Escher

This book is a great achievement in developing a change in attitude and approach towards hearing voices.

This book is for voice hearers and the people they select to support them. It will enable people who have difficulties to cope with their voices and to discover different sides to their voices. Following a systematic approach it will unfold their relation with the voices and by doing so will stimulate them to acquire more effective ways of coping. Most important in this process, and well stimulated in this workbook, is to take ownership of the experience from writing one's own life history in relation to ones voices. Becoming more curious about the voices is stimulated by the questions and promotes ownership as well.

This book stimulates you to plan ones own life again, this is especially helpful for those who are feeling to overpowered by the voices to become their master.

In social fields and in medical care hearing voices is seen as the consequence of mental illness. Voices are felt only to be very negative, and must be controlled by professionals. Voices are hardly ever interpreted as the messengers of the persons life history.

This book however helps a person to overcome three handicaps:
1) The idea that hearing voices is the consequence of an existing illness within the person, most likely being schizophrenia, an illness of unknown origin.
2) The idea that schizophrenia is a diagnosis of an illness not related in an understandable manner with the life history of that person.
3) The idea that the person as the consequence of the illness concept is powerless against the voices, that the voices are not owned by the person, while in fact the voices are a persons own experience understandable from the personal trauma's or overpowering problems with life.

Let us first explain how Psychiatry came to look at hearing voices. It has already been 100 years since Kraeplin formulated the concept of 'illness entities' in clinical psychiatry. In this concept all symptoms are seen as the results of an existing illness within the person of which the origin is still unknown. Science in the meantime has proven that the construct of an existing illness entity is not valid. Schizophrenia for instance is a construct that represents a broad range of complaints shown by very different persons (Bentall 1990, Boyle 1990 etc. etc.).

Schizophrenia does not represent a diagnosis. In a diagnosis one tries to understand what has led up to the complaints.One analyses the complex interaction between the persons capacities, the personal development and social conditions's/he is living in.

The term schizophrenia, in the classification system as used in the DSM, represents a category based upon a rather broad range of available symptoms at a certain moment or period in time. This period does not tell us anything about the possible causes nor does it include the personal experiences and their meaning for the person involved. Neither does it indicate how to cope with the experience.

Calling a person who cannot cope with the voices 'ill' is understandable when the voices and the emotions or behaviour they provoke are dominating the persons functioning and life. It is reasonable to call the person 'ill' when the voices are not an integrated part of the person but destroy ones free will. It is not right however to look at hearing voices in itself as a symptom of an illness. No it is the coping with that experience that might give rise to the emotions and behaviour that can be called ill.

Therefore a person who hears voices but cannot cope with them, needs support to overcome the powerlessness and to be able to begin living again. Support is needed in coping with voices, Support is also needed in order to become stronger in ones own identity. Lastly support is needed in accepting that what has happened has happened and should not be felt guilty about rather it needs to be placed back in the life history, placing the responsibility where it belongs with the activist not the recipient.

It is the great merit of Ron Coleman that he has seen these three handicaps in his own life and with great persistence has changed his life. Becoming a victor after having been a victim. He did not deny what has happened to him, but became critical in a way that made it possible to build his own life. His second great merit is that he found companions in the mental health professional world.It is the vision of Mike Smith that has seen the value of Rons' work and has joined with him to follow this different road. They wrote in partnership this fantastic book. It is a great opportunity that Mike and Ron have worked together to develop this practical support system for those voice hearers who intend to build up their own life. Not denying the hard work to come but commencing on the road instead of waiting for some coming wonder. This book is based upon our research as far as overcoming the first handicap is concerned, It is based on Rons' private experience as far as the second and third handicaps are concerned. It is however further based upon the experience of many other voice hearers met in support groups in the U.K. These people have taught Mike and Ron to ask the right questions. it is based on experience, not yet on scientific evaluation.

Romme & Escher 1997.

Introduction to the Second Edition

It is hard for us to believe that seven years have passed since the first edition of Working with Voices was written. The workbook has in this time been translated into fourteen languages and has been received enthusiastically in many countries. In the United Kingdom alone the book has been reprinted nine times and there has been a temptation on our part to just continue with reprinting. Both of us however have agreed that the first edition as good as it was for the time it was written is now no longer reflective of how we have moved on indeed how the world of understanding voices has moved and we decided it was time to completely re-write the work. The background is in essence the same in 2004 as it was in 1997 as are the principles of working with people. It is clear to us that what has changed is our own and others experience of working with people who hear voices and that over the last seven years voice hearers have taught us a great deal that we believe will be useful to others.

In this, the second edition of Working with Voices we have taken a slightly different approach to both how we gather information about someone's voice hearing experience and more importantly what we do with that information and how we use it to form an action plan that keeps the voice hearer at the centre of the process. In this edition we have tried to identify the gaps in the first edition and rectify them by using the numerous evaluations and comments we have received from those who have used the workbook to inform and guide this edition. We have no doubt that this edition will also be subject to scrutiny by both ourselves' and others' and time will once again cause us to make further changes. We believe that if the time ever comes when there are no more changes to be made (in our opinion) then it would probably mean it is time for us to give up working with voices.

This edition has also been designed in such a way to allow practitioners to be more effective in their own practice, whilst retaining the voice hearers' position of being in control of the process and more importantly their own experiences.

P&P
PRESS LTD

How the workbook is structured

This edition has been structured in a different way from the fist edition there are two main reasons for this these are:

1. Over the years many clients and professionals have either written to us or spoke with us about how they have used the workbook not following it the way we wrote it but using the workbook in a way that made sense to the client. When we explored this with them there was a clear pattern that emerged that suggested to us that although the content of the workbook was right the way we had laid out the workbook did not reflect how it was being used. Discussions between ourselves showed that we also did not follow the structure of the first edition and that independently of each other we were following the same process.

2. It is now clear to us that the main weakness of the first edition is the lack of space in which to create an action plan that can be used by both the voice hearer and the worker that enables the voice hearer to move much beyond identifying, exploring and understanding their experience. If you like we created in the first edition a methodology that allowed the voice hearer to stop being a victim without giving them the tools to enable them to complete their victory.

Working through the Workbook

As always it is important that we follow a process when we work either with someone who hears voices or are working through our own voice hearing experience. It is through the process of identifying your experience, exploring the experience, understanding the experience for yourself and then making choices about how you go forward. This is in effect the process that allows us to reclaim our lives and become victors over our experiences rather than victims of it or in it.

Ground rules

- Voices are real, pointless arguments about whom they are real for, are by definition, pointless!

- Voices in themselves may not be the problem rather relationships with them, the power they have and their influence in a persons' life may be the problem.

- This book belongs to the voice hearer, it should be a record of their experience, their coping and their plans for the future

- It is all right for new coping strategies to be slow to work.

- Many people try different ways of dealing with the voices. It is better to try and partially succeed than to never to try at all. You are in charge as long as you try. You are no longer the victim you are now the victor.

- Take your time there are no prizes for finishing quickly.

Who should use this workbook?

This book can help most people who are willing to ask themselves a few questions about their voices. Acknowledging the reality of your experience then gives you permission to do something about it. There are different phases of the voice hearing experience that are well described by Romme & Escher, in the first, startling phase when you are often afraid of your voices or they may confuse you it may help to first get some power and influence over your voices by learning some simple short term coping strategies, however we have found that even at times when you are afraid of or unclear about your voices, this book by helping you to start to recognise them as entities and understand your relationships with them and their influence upon your life can be helpful. The second, Organising phase, is an ideal time to use the whole of the book in depth, by following the path of those who have gone before you can make many short cuts in organising your experience in a more helpful way. Finally during the stabilisation phase you can also use this book to plan where you want to go, how you want things to change and who can you recruit to help you.

Who shouldn't use the workbook?

People who deny the experience or whose anxiety is so great that to even begin to explore the experience would be ultimately more harmful (not many people fit into this group and you can learn to manage your fears and anxieties first)

Why should I use this workbook?

There are three main things that you can do with this book.

-The first is to be clear about your experiences and share them with others if you choose to do so.

-The second is to explore how you cope and to build upon this, there are many things that you can learn especially from other people who hear voices and do not often become unwell

The third thing is to resolve to move on with your experiences and to reclaim your life following this framework

Basic information

Although we talk about voices throughout we believe that you can mostly apply these principles to visions (seeing voices as we like to sometimes think) and other unusual experiences like feeling or smelling things, if these other experiences are true to you then substitute the words.

Hearing voices does not mean you are sick or ill 4% of the population hear voices, voice hearing is however commoner amongst people who are labelled as mentally ill and so we have little doubt that voices in themselves may not be the problem but they can for some people cause them to have problems that might be described as "Illnesses" Voice hearing in itself is not generally the problem for most people we meet although it may contribute to your problems. Often it is your relationship with your voices, how you interpret them, what they make you believe and how they effect or interfere with your life that may lead to you feeling that you need help, the metaphor illness may be helpful at times in your life but also it can in itself be the problem. Once you are determined to be ill it can be hard to live your life instead of your label and it is certainly hard to prove that you are not ill.

Following a process that helps you reclaim your life!

This book follows a process that many people have described as their natural response to reclaiming their life after being diagnosed as ill and being troubled by unusual experiences. Mike has researched this process and has written widely about it and Ron has lived it. We both believe that recovery is a personal concept and is a journey rather than an event. That said however we believe that as a journey there can be short cuts, there are different routes you can follow and there are people and places along the road that can be positive and negative. We have a rather simple view of recovery, which is "reclaiming your life", so we do not believe that you have to stop hearing voices to recover nor do we believe that there is a right and wrong way, just different paths that lead you to the same place.

The process

Identifying your experiences

Identifying your experiences in your own words and as you see them . Many people do not fully know, nor are able to share their voice hearing experience, often realising that you are not alone with this experience can be beneficial and recognising for yourself what you are dealing with and putting it into perspective can help.

Exploring your experiences

Looking in depth at your experiences and looking beyond yourself to others and their reactions. We will also look at the relationships you have with your voices, the influence they have over you and how it affects you living your life and what control you do or do not have. This may be the first time you have explored your experiences. This travelling of new ground can be hard both for you and the person who is working with you. I hope it can completely change the way you and others around you view your experiences.

Understanding your experiences

This is for you, and with your permission a chosen person, to begin to understand and to put into context your experiences. It aims to clarify your beliefs and to help you make decisions about how you want to move forward together.

Moving on

This phase is about accepting if you want to, and making choices about how you want to cope and live with your voices. It is also about developing strategies for you to take control in your life and for some getting back your life as you want it. There are a number of coping mechanisms and strategies you can acquire from other people and there is no right way, just the way for you today. This can involve developing an action plan to deal with your experience. Most professionals are required to plan and record what they do for you. You can use this to help you, if you choose, when working with professionals. This plan should be focused around your experiences and how you understand them, and should work to your goals-nobody else's.

P&P
PRESS LTD

What do you want from this Workbook?

Often when we work through issues around voices we start by identifying the problem, in this edition of the workbook we have turned this on its head and will start by looking at what you want from the process. This is because we have concluded that having dreams and objectives at the beginning of the process gives us a much greater incentive to move forward. Once you know your dreams it is our hope that by working through the workbook you will end up developing an action plan that will allow you to take control of your experience and to live your life.

Creating your Future

There are numerous ways in which you can start planning your goals for the future, we would suggest that you use a technique called mapping. Mapping is a technique that allows you to explore in a focused way where you want to be in your life, how you will get there, what you need to get there, who you need to help you get there and what the pitfalls on your journey might be, we will walk through this at the end of the book.

DREAMS

Close your eyes and think about what you want to achieve by working through this workbook. Spend at least 30 minutes simply thinking about where you want to be in your life. Write this here.

Then ask yourself what would be realistic to achieve in one years' time. It might help to think about some of the following questions.

"I will live in"

"I will be with"

"I will be doing"

"These are the kinds of things I'd be doing"

"I will be feeling"

These are my Goals for the next year.

Having goals are crucial if you want to move forward in a positive way. If you don't then your reality will fall short of what is possible for you. By doing this you may not achieve all of your goals, but you will get closer.

NIGHTMARE

Close your eyes and think about all the things in your life that have caused you pain, distress, anger and frustration. These things could be brought to the fore as you work through the workbook so it is useful that you write them down so that they do not take you by surprise later in the process. These can be states of mind as well as actual occurrences and symptoms of your mental health problems.

Be honest will help you and those around you to navigate through
your journey in a way that will either avoid pitfalls or ensure you are prepared for
them if and when they happen.

You might want to write about how you feel in situations that affect you such as working, being with people, travelling, being on your own or how you feel at different times of the day, week or even year. It might be useful to use the just heard voices for the next ten days before you complete this section. (This can be found on the next two pages.)

Write about your fears of the process here.

Identifying your experiences

Firstly, your voices are real! Arguing about whether they exist or not is pointless, annoying, and can become the problem in itself. In order to help you we must acknowledge the reality of your experience.

Lets look at the voices that you currently hear!

Have you tried to find the source of the voices, where they come from, do you have an explanation, is there a different explanation for each voice? Please write down your thoughts here.

If you are unsure and you have someone about you that you can trust you could always try asking your voices the question directly, we describe this later in the section on interviewing voices/ voice dialogues but for now lets continue with the basics.

The basics, focussing on your voice/s

By starting with the very basics of voices it can help you to recognise the reality of the experience and begin if necessary to own it because when you own the experience it becomes your responsibility to deal with it! Having some basic knowledge of your experience is known to generally reduce your anxiety about them. We will look here at very basic things about the nature of the experience and nothing at all about content so if you are afraid of your voices don't worry.

- Are you hearing voices now?   Yes/No

- Where are they in room?

- Do you see them as well?   Yes/No/Sometimes

- Are they the same gender as you?   Yes/No/Mixed

- How are they speaking, loud or quiet?

- Are they distinct separate voices, mumblings or crowds?

- Are these voices coming from you or something else?   Me/ Something else

If you are unclear or have difficulties identifying your voices or talking about them try completing the next page for each time you hear a voice, keep a record for a week.

"I've just heard voices" checklist

Now complete these next two pages each time you hear voices for the next 7 days at least. Feel free to photocopy these two pages.

Date .... Time spent with voices ....

Time .... Time with voices voluntarily ....

Please be as honest as possible as this checklist is to help you identify the voices, and any things which occur that can help you to identify when the voices communicate with you, and to develop ways of predicting and organising your life to accommodate the voices.

The voices I heard were:

1..   4..

2..   5..

3..   6..

The voices said

· I Felt

· I was at (Place)

- I was with (Company)

- I was doing

- The place was (Noisy, quiet, people talking)

- Before the voices came I had been thinking about

Please answer the following yes or no
- My state of consciousness was altered   Yes/No
- My Vision was heightened/altered   Yes/No
- I felt Paranoid   Yes/No
- I felt out of control   Yes/No
- I felt powerful   Yes/No

My explanation for why I just heard voices is:

OK now lets write down some of the characteristics of your voices

- Do you hear clear voices or sounds or music or crowds of people or do you hear mumbling or blurred conversations?

- Are these voices/sounds your own voice or another person's voice?

For example if they are another person's voice do they reflect how you are feeling?

- If you are unhappy do voices punish you?

- If you are happy do voices encourage you?

- When you feel vulnerable do voices threaten you?

- When you feel good do voices go away or have little influence on you?

If it is your own voice that you clearly hear then this is not directly considered to be an hallucination and it is known as a Syntonic experience, therefore it is important to be clear how you hear the voice. Many people however hear their own thoughts and feelings but the voice is not them, this is called a Dystonic experience.

How do you hear the voice?

- Is it clear words?

- Is it thoughts that are inserted?

- Is it Telepathic communication?

- Is it other people's feelings and thoughts that you are sensitive to feel?

Another way? If so please explain

- Do you hear the voices through your ears or some other way? Is it through your ears, elsewhere in the body e.g. stomach, is it direct into mind through telepathy?

- Can other people hear these sounds, if not what is your explanation for this?

- Can your voices influence you, for example stopping you doing something or keeping you awake? We will look in detail at this later.

- Do you hear good or bad voices, are they neutral or is it all of them?

- How often do you hear voices, are there any patterns you have noticed?

- If you are unsure the next section may help you.

Exploring your experiences

In this section we want to go further and look not just at your current experiences but how they have changed over time and what has helped you.

- How long have you heard voices?

- When did they first start, how old were you?

- How long have you been hearing voices?

- Have other people told you that you are ill? If so what diagnosis have they given you?

- Do you feel ill?

- Do you agree with you diagnosis?

Don't worry if you disagree or your diagnosis has changed, this is pretty normal and diagnosis is not always accurate but it is important to recognise, if you disagree or agree it can affect you in many ways that actually can become problems for you, we will look at his later.

First voice hearing experience and circumstances related to it

Lets go back to the beginning, 27% of young people who hear voices say that they have always heard voices, is this true for you?   yes/no

- If you have always heard voices when did these voices become a problem for you?

- What was happening in your life at this time?

- If No at what age did you start to hear any voices good or bad?

- What year was this and how old were you?

Time line for voice hearing

TIME LINE GRAPH FOR .... **TO.** ... / .. / **20.**

Once the person has described their current situation it might be helpful to ask generalised, open ended questions that help build up a picture of who the person is and the various events and influences that they see as having been significant in their lives.

This **DOES NOT** at this stage need to be a complex and detailed piece of work, but will again enable the person to clarify issues affecting them. It can also provide the person with a useful pivot from which they can begin a move forward from the assessment to the 'action planning'.
Include known facts about the person into the Time Line - acknowledge the past with the person!

- Look back at the first experience, can you remember it, where were you, describe it.

- How did you react, what did you do, whom did you tell, what were their reactions, if you told no one why?

- What led up to the experience describe it, had there been significant things happening in your life i.e. loss of a loved one, abuse of yourself? Romme & Escher (1997) wrote of the following being just some of the life events that they were commonly told of.

- Possible events leading to first voice hearing experience

Death	Birth in family
Love	Unreturned love
First menstruation	First sexual experiences
Others illness	After I did something
Divorce	Witnessing a single trauma
Failure in a course or study	Being mentally ill
Going into hospital	Being detained
Being tortured	Pregnancy
Using drugs	Relationship breakdown
Violence between parents	Religious or spiritual crisis

Lets now move on to your current voices.

- How often do you now hear voices?

- Are you mostly more powerful than your voices or does it vary, please describe it?

- Do they come at certain times of the day, are you more vulnerable to them at certain times, if so when?

- Where are they mostly in the room, are they close or distant?

- Do you know who they are, do you have an identity for them or do they remind you of someone?

- Do you have a voice that is more dominant or significant than the rest, if so do you know who it is?

It can be helpful to list your voices or to give them names in order that you can create a better understanding of how they influence your life and who they are, fill in the following table.

Influence of the voices

Look again at your voices but in more depth, look at the first voice hearing experience and how it has changed, for some people this can be important.

Original voice profile (OVP)

Identity of each voice or name	
When did you 1st hear it (age)	
In what circumstances	
Age approx. of voice	
How does it make you feel	
What it says	
How it influences your life	

Now record your voices as they are now noting any changes that have occurred since you started hearing voices.

Current voice profile (CVP)

Identity of each voice or name	
When did you 1st hear it (age)	
In what circumstances-stances	
Age approx. of voice	
How does it make you feel	
What it says	
How it influences your life	

From the above table write down what are the main influences that your voices have on your life, feeling special for example or feeling suspicious.

Is your consciousness altered before or during the voice hearing, do you feel out of control, experience flashbacks or lose time, if you are unsure you can use a questionnaire called the Dissociative Experience Scale (DES Putnam & Bernstein) which identifies if this change in consciousness is in itself a problem for you.

- Do your voices confuse you?

- Do your voices have power over you?

- Do they try to get you to do things that you don't want to do?

If yes how do they do this?

Can you resist them, if so how do you do this?
Be honest with yourself, many voice hearers don't realise that they do, mostly resist their voices commands or suggestions and it is important to realise how you do this. If you are unsure ask yourself the following questions in the table

Resisting commands/orders/requests

A	How often do voices try to get me to do something?	
B	How often do I actually do what they order or ask me to do	
	Why is there a difference between A & B, how do I resist, deny orders, what makes it easy/ hard	

- Do you do bargains with your voices? Write down how you do this.

Triggers for voices

Many people have told us that their voices are triggered by specific emotions events or places. The following are some examples of what people have told us. It is important that you and others know of these triggers because you can then avoid your personal triggers, anticipate or understand it if you cant avoid it and hopefully be more able to take control of events.

Have you noticed that the voices are present when you feel certain emotions?

Emotional triggers

Happy	Sad
Grief	Insecurity
Arousal	Suspicion
Jealously	Guilt
Despair	My anger
Relief	Hate
Boredom	Stress

Write about the feelings you have to deal with when your voices are at their worst.

P&P
PRESS LTD

Write about the feelings you have to deal with when your voices are at their most positive.

If like many people your emotional response to your voices is anger make sure you tell people about this. This can stop people seeing your anger as a symptom and demonstrate to yourself and others that the emotion is reactive.

Use this space to write about other ways you are affected emotionally by your voices.

Event triggers

Mark triggers that apply to you or add new ones in the blank boxes.

Suspicious	Being in crowds
Anniversaries	Sex
Sounds	Sexual approaches to other to you
Smells	Being alone
Out at night	Going to bed
Violence of others	Being threatened/bullied
Having nothing to do	Changing consciousness (daydreams)
Having too much to do	Work
Death	World events
Being vulnerable	Not being believed

Looking at the above you can decide what are the things that trigger your voices or give them some power and can give you some warning too prepare yourself. When you are aware of this you can anticipate certain voices and situations and prepare yourself to be more strong or less vulnerable, we will look at this in coping with voices where we call it anticipating voices and also resisting orders. What are your warning signs?

My Triggers (Warning signs)

My Relationship with my voices

We now need to look at the relationships you have with your voices. As we have said elsewhere voices are not usually in themselves the problem, rather it is the relationship you have with them, their influence on your life and the degree of control and power they or you have from time to time that is commonly the problem. If it applies to you Please answer the following questions and add as much detail as possible?

• Does voice hearing frighten you? If so explain how

• Does it leave you powerless? If so explain how

• Do you try to deny it is happening? If so explain how

- Does it make you feel unwell, crazy or mad? If so explain how

- Can you have a 2-way dialogue with your voices? If so explain how

- Can you command them? If so explain how

- Can you bargain and do deals with them? If so explain how

- Do they have special powers? If so explain how

- Can they influence your thinking or actions? If so explain how

- Do you trust your voices? If so explain how

The support or influence of others

We know that those people who have friends, allies and family about them, generally find it easier to cope than those who feel alone with their voices and so it can help for us and others trying to help to look at who is around you and who helps and how with their voice hearing?

· Who knows about your voices?

· Can you talk with these people openly about your voices and what do they think, if you are unsure ask them?

For many people the real problems that they come to understand is not the voices that they hear but the fact that they are alone with the voices so have no other point of view to help them or that they have no one they can honestly ask about the voices. Try filling in the following section to see how much help you can get from others with your voices.

My social network

Name	Do they know about the voices?	Can you talk with them about the voices? How much do they know? What has been their reaction? What would you like them to do?

P&P
PRESS LTD

Having a trialogue with voices (for friends, carers or people supporting a person who hears voices)

Can you speak reasonably with your voices, many people have not tried and some are too afraid of their voices to try, if this is the case then we have found that others who aren't as afraid or influenced by your voices can sometimes have a reasonable relationship with your voices. We would suggest being sensible and using the following questions as a starting point, once a dialogue starts you may wish to ask new questions that are not written here depending upon what the voices tell you.

Of course the person asking the questions can not hear the response and so the voice hearer will have to relay what the voice replies hence a trialogue, but we have found that interviewers can ask questions direct to most voices, occasionally the voice hearer may also have to relay a question to a voice that does not hear direct questions. . In order to have a trialogue you have to remember it is at least a three way process of equals (both of us have had discussions with more than one voice at a time, so it can become quite confusing if you don't keep to simple rules of clarifying who is saying what). Do not argue aggressively with voices, threaten them or disrespect them, we have found it gets you nowhere.

The purpose of the dialogue is to gather further information for the person to better understand, but also to help the person. Looking at the OVP and the CVP you should have some information already about many of the persons voices, if you want to start with some basic questions some of the following may help to start.

1. Will you speak with me?
2. Who are you, do you have a name?
3. Are you male or female?
4. Are you a person or another type of entity?
5. How long have you been with this person?
6. When did you come into their life?
7. Why are you in this persons life
8. What role do you play in their life? Are you helping or causing problems
9. Why do you speak to them
10. How would you describe the person you speak to?

Looking at the CVP you may wish to ask certain voices questions, an example we will give is with a voice that causes people dilemmas in this example a suicide voice. It is not uncommon for people to hear voices that tell them to kill themselves. We have found that if you ask the person why the voice has influence and upsets them they can be unclear or vague, asking the voice directly can help you to understand the person and the voice better.

eg.

"You tell Mark each day to kill himself, why should he do this?"

"Is it because you (the voice) want to die?"

"What will happen to you if he does kill himself?"

With Mark you want him to have more power and his voice to have less influence and so a discussion with his voices will try to remove some of the their power or their ability to influence him and so the discussion should be facilitated this way, the only way we have found to do this is to treat the voice as if it were a person in the room with you and to think and question as if it was happening this way.

P&P PRESS LTD

- Do you have beliefs that other people think are unusual but are related to the voices that you hear? e.g. some people believe that they are communicating with spirits, others think that they may have a special purpose in life and others do not agree with you.

- Do you do certain things as a result of your beliefs; do you look for your voices, stop going out, tell others etc?

- Do you deny or ignore your voices?

- How would you describe your relationship with your voices now, are they positive, negative, both or neutral?

- Can they influence what you do?

- Can you resist or ignore them? (See resisting voices earlier on)

- Are some of them more influential than others?

How have you coped

We have found that many people can learn to cope and live with the voices that they hear if this is what they want to do. We will list here just a small selection of coping strategies for voice hearing experiences if you want to see a more extensive list see the book edited by Mike Smith called Psychiatric first aid also available from **P&P press.**

What ways of coping have you tried and found helpful, the following are some brief examples:

- Ways of distracting you, hobbies, meeting friends, telephoning, exercise, drowning them out, playing music etc.

- Ways of changing your thinking, thinking methods, allowing positive voices, structuring time and giving time to your voices, checking out what's real etc.

- Changing what you do, avoid stress, keep a diary, talk to friends, treating yourself etc.

- Answering back, using drugs prescribed and other, using earplugs, noise generators.

Understanding your experience

Now its time to start to come to some understanding about what your experiences have been, how they fit into your life, why you hear voices, what are your beliefs about this in order that you can make some choices about moving on.

Life history

What is your life history? List those things that have happened to you that you think may be relevant to why you now hear voices, if you are unsure, write down the events and feelings through your life and how they have formed you as you now are, this will help you to some understanding of your experiences.

LIFE HISTORY In my Words by ....

LIFE HISTORY in my words by ....

Taking your life history. Look back at it, especially at the critical events, how are these things related to why you now hear voices, did it change your relationship, did it cause the voices to come, did it give them more power, do they abuse you because of it?

With the critical events it helps to understand the importance of these events in your life, and how do they now contribute to the person you are.

Many people relate their voices to traumatic life events (anywhere from 25-95%), however it is helpful to understand why this is so. For example many people tell of childhood sexual abuse being important or witnessing a trauma, what we are interested in is how this has affected you for instance do your voice blame you, do you feel guilty or ashamed has it affected your ability to trust others etc. We call this creating an Ego document, you simply look at the life events that you may have listed in your life history and ask yourself, Well why are these events important? For example why is my Fathers death important, was it because I never said goodbye, was it because I wanted him to see the person I have become, was it because I feel responsible for his death or his feelings when he died?

My Life

Life Event	Why it is important, how it now makes me think feel and behave

P&P
PRESS LTD

Have you started to organise your experiences, and create an understanding of them?

Do you know why you hear voices; do you now have an explanation for them? Don't worry if your explanation changes over time, most people find that as they meet new people and have more experiences they develop a better understanding of themselves and vary their opinions.

Is your explanation generally helpful? For some people it is the explanation for the voices that can lead them to be seen as ill, i.e. if others cannot accept your explanation, they may call this a "Delusion". It always helps to have a clear understanding because this makes people less likely to think your ideas are bizarre and more able to have an honest dialogue with you that can help you further adapt your beliefs.

What is your explanation for your voices?

What are the real problems for you?

AS we have discussed the problem is not likely to be the voices but the influence that they on your life, the power that they have over you or what they make you do. You can look through what you have written, the "I've just heard voices checklist" etc. to help you to conclude this.

Moving on/ Action Planning

Giving up voices and indeed giving up madness can be a very difficult thing to do, you should not deny your own history but you should acknowledge it and make choices to move on in your life

Planning is essential use the next few pages to create a plan for the next year get people you need to sign up to your plan then just do it.

P&P PRESS LTD

Referring back to your dreams what do you want to happen over the next twelve months?

Describe the situation now

Who are you going to involve in order to achieve the things you want to happen over the next twelve months?

What other things do you need to make this happen?
E.g. money

What needs to have happened in six months?

What needs to have happened in three months?

What do you need to do over the next month?

What do you need to do tomorrow?

NOTES

NOTES

NOTES

NOTES